Steam Motive Power Centres

No.5: NEWCASTLE

Including: Newcastle Central and Gateshead Motive Power Depot

INTRODUCTION

Newcastle Central station was once a mecca for railway enthusiasts, both locally and nationally. Behind the grandeur of its' Neo Classical frontage lies a superbly designed array of platforms carrying passengers, parcels and mail from arriving and departing trains and those passing through this iconic northern city.

During the 1950s and the 1960s Newcastle Central station drew many a crowd of eager enthusiasts including Ian Falcus, Howard Forster, Bill Hampson, Bob Payne, Alan Thompson, Chris Campbell and the late Frank Coulton, who devoted their weekends to the documentation of every locomotive that passed by the blinking eye of their cameras.

The first section of this album is a presentation of their photographic work from the period 1951-1964. Prolific in content, evidencing numerous classes of engines hauling trains predominantly to and from the English and Scottish capitals with the addition of Hexham, Carlisle, Hawick and Consett from the west end of the station and Alnwick, the coast, South Shields, Sunderland and Middlesbrough from the east.

The second part of the album documents Gateshead MPD from 1963-1965 in the run down to the end of steam including some unusual and precariously taken photographs. All the images at 52A are the work of the late Frank Coulton, a private and well respected steam enthusiast and good friend.

Frank was a prolific railway modeller who started off building basic models from scratch in the mid 1950s. When he decided he would develop and hone his building skills he would search high and low for accurate images of the locomotives he was wanting to construct. Frustrated by poor quality and inconsistent images he began to hunt out the real thing and photograph them himself. After missing the withdrawn LNER G5s which he was modelling by two years, he realised that he didn't want to miss an engine again. Consequently, he photographed everything in all weathers and at all times providing an invaluable and rare personal archive. Modern technology means we can clean up these visual gems and show Franks' vision off at its best.

I know that Frank was something of a permanent fixture around the Gateshead and Bensham area. The fact that he had a line-side permit means that we are now treated to a collection of images taken from otherwise 'off-limits' locations. I hope you enjoy this collection as much as I have in compiling it.

With special thanks to Mark Williams for his technical assistance and a thankyou to all contributors.

David Dunn, Cramlington. September 2008

Printed and bound by The Amadeus Press, Cleckheaton, West Yorkshire
First published in the United Kingdom by Book Law Publications, 382 Carlton Hill, Nottingham, NG4 1JA

A picturesque image of the elegantly shaped W.Worsdell Gateshead built North Eastern Railway Class R, LNER D20 No.62387 of Heaton shed, with a modified flush-sided NER tender, about to depart with empty stock to Heaton carriage sidings on 5th July 1957. Under the arching ribs of the station roof can be seen a selection of hoardings advertising local stores and newspapers, and of course a sight unseen today, one for Capstan cigarettes. *H.Forster.*

(Title page) A perfectly framed, picturesque image of Thompson B1 No.61222 of Carlisle Canal shed, leaving platform 14 on 20th November 1954 with the 12.20 p.m. to Carlisle, overlooked by the spire of St. Mary's Cathedral. *I.Falcus.*

On Friday 6th September 1963 A4 No.60019 BITTERN had charge of a Scarborough—Glasgow train and is nicely steamed up prior to leaving Central for the north. The external condition of the locomotive is nothing less than deplorable and somewhat typical of the way Gateshead turned out its premier steam motive power but the Pacific was soon to transferred to Aberdeen where Ferryhill shed took a more benevolent attitude to cleaning its charges. Nevertheless the A4 still makes a stirring sight. *F.Coulton*.

BR Standard Class 2MT No.78046 of Hawick shed, about to leave from platform 12 at Newcastle's west end with the 4.27 p.m. Newcastle—Hawick. The date is 9th May 1956 and the 2-6-0 is one of a pair (78047 was the other) allocated to 64G from new during the previous October; two more were to follow, 78049 in June 1959 and 78048 in July 1960. Note the Hawick duty number 279 - did Hawick really have that many duties! - on the footplate centre lamp bracket, and the BR 2MT classification on the buffer beam. These engines were to prove very popular with the enginemen, especially during the harsh winter months over the more remote sections of Waverley line which linked Hawick with the rest of the world. *H.Forster.*

Four days earlier D49/1 No.62733 NORTHUMBERLAND of Edinburgh Haymarket shed, had charge of the 4.27 p.m. Newcastle–Hawick. This engine was fitted with an ex Great Central tender. *H.Forster.*

A pair of bunker to bunker Fairburn 2-6-4Ts Nos.42094 and 42073 working a special train to Sunderland on 3rd March 1956. Originally Standard 4MTs 80031-3 were to be allocated to the North Eastern Region, but were deemed to be 'out of gauge' at Middlesbrough roundhouse and were instead sent to the Southern Region. In return these two Fairburns were transferred to the North East as a trial; No.42073 in October 1954 and No.42094 during the following December. They were allocated to Gateshead rather than Middlesbrough and although the 'trial' was apparently proved to be unsuccessful, they were not transferred away to Manningham shed until June 1957, some two and a half years later. During its time at 52A No.42073 upset the authorities somewhat when on the 19th April 1955 it collided with V2 No.60968 on the crossing at the east end of Central station, knocking the 2-6-2 onto its side. *H.Forster.*

Another unusual sighting at Central, this one on 29th May 1958, was that of Ivatt class 2MT No.46400 of Sheffield Millhouses shed. Passing behind the back of the station, the 2-6-0 has charge of a Down goods bound for Heaton. This engine was probably on a running-in turn after being repaired at either Darlington or Gateshead works. *H.Forster.*

A pair of Gresley V3 2-6-2 tanks Nos.67691 and 67654, both of Heaton, bringing the Up service of THE NORSEMAN into Central station on Saturday 10th May 1958. This train had origins back in the heady days of a publicity driven LNER when on 16th June 1928 the Saturdays Only boat train from King's Cross to the newly opened Tyne Commission Quay ran direct for the first time. The new facilities on the Tyne allowed trains to run onto the quay so that passengers for the Norway bound ferry could step from train to ship - well virtually. The summer sailings and the trains became popular and in June 1931 the LNER bestowed the name THE NORSEMAN on the SO train but although the coach roof boards carried the full title, the locomotive headboard had just NORSEMAN. Wartime saw the service disappear from the timetables and resumption did not take place until 1946 when only through coaches were hauled to Newcastle by certain expresses from King's Cross and the 2-6-2T took over for the short journey to the Quay. However, in 1950 the through trains were reintroduced in both Up and Down directions and the service became year round. A new headboard with prefix was cast and faster schedules introduced. THE NORSEMAN was back in business. Although Pacific hauled between London and Newcastle, the rather arduous and awkward leg from Central to Tyne Commission Quay was always in the hands of two robust tanks engines; A5s served from 1928 until 1938 when the V1 class took over. Note that the express headcode was used throughout although the headboard was probably with the Pacific which would take over from these two. Just visible in the background to the left, was a DMU set on a Newcastle—Carlisle service. *H.Forster.*

9

An evocative steam filled shot of BR Standard Class 3MT No.77014 of Blaydon shed, arriving at platform 8 with empty stock from Scotswood Bridge carriage sidings on Saturday 27th October 1956. Just above the engine can be seen what appears to be a signal gantry arm being dismantled using block and tackle pulleys. On platform 8 is a steel fabrication to which a rope has been attached from scaffolding alongside the gantry arm. There seems to be no means of cordoning off the area where the work is being carried out nor is there any warning signs of any sort! Today that whole area of platform would have been surrounded by hoarding and, most probably the platform road would have been taken out of use, especially whilst the work was being undertaken above the trains but this is 1956 and the work was part of the resignalling of the station. The unidentified A8 4-6-2T hiding in the background was bound for Middlesbrough. *H.Forster.*

Thompson A2/1 Pacific No.60509 WAVERLEY of Haymarket shed, heads the Up HEART OF MIDLOTHIAN on Saturday 5th May 1956. It was quite unusual to have a Thompson Pacific hauling this train as it was normally a top link Haymarket Peppercorn A1 turn. However, the A2 is nicely turned out and it was not just ex works gloss either because No.60509 had not been to Doncaster 'Plant' since the previous January so, it was all down to the Haymarket cleaners and what a superb job they have done. Lets hope the engine performed as good as it looked. *H.Forster.*

The closure of all three West Coast routes into Carlisle, due to flooding and a landslide, on the 29th and 30th October 1954, afforded lucky spotters the rare chance to witness the first recorded appearance in Newcastle, of a Stanier Pacific. Polmadie based No.46232 DUCHESS OF MONTROSE was returning home after working a diverted Glasgow (Central)—London (Euston) sleeping car express into Newcastle. The 'Duchess' was working a fitted freight of vans and container flats with the nearest van to the tender carrying a temporary poster signifying it was carrying Huntley & Palmers biscuits. Another 'Duchess' arriving from the north that day was No.46221 QUEEN ELIZABETH on the Up ROYAL SCOT which was handed over to V2 No.60981 for the rest of that trains journey south from Newcastle. No.46230 DUCHESS OF BUCCLEUCH also visited Newcastle along with a handful of other 'foreigners' including a couple of 'Royal Scots', and 'Jubilees'. Just visible on the left of the picture is the Newcastle No.1 signal box, straddling the tracks in typical NER style, on a gantry. *H.Forster.*

Hawick shed was not adverse to using other depots charges on its 'numerous' duties so it is no surprise to see Blaydon based Standard Class 4MT No.76046 hauling the 4.27 p.m. Newcastle—Hawick in this 24th September 1955 view of the west end of the station. Another Blaydon engine, V3 No.67653 was working empty stock to Blaydon carriage sidings but it would be missed by the crowd of spotters as the Hawick train masked its exit. The splendid signal gantry and silhouette of St Mary's Cathedral to the left, complete the shot. *H.Forster.* 13

Not just a magnificent photograph but somewhat unique because it shows the rare combination of double-heading north out of Newcastle. Also, Peppercorn Pacifics and Gresley V2s were not seen working together everyday, especially with 2-6-2 inside. A2 No.60538 VELOCITY of Gateshead and Heaton V2 No.60910 are about to make a spirited journey north on 30th July 1955 with the Saturdays Only (summer service) Filey—Edinburgh. Crates of milk on platform 9 await collection by the kitchen staff of a southbound express. *H.Forster.*

J72 No.68680 of Gateshead shed, resplendent in mixed traffic livery as station pilot on 16th May 1959. In August 1937 it was decided by the LNER hierarchy that two Gateshead J72s, after being fitted with vacuum ejectors and carriage warming apparatus, were to be used as station pilots at Newcastle. They were then afforded full passenger livery and kept clean, being constantly in the public eye. Originally numbered No.1720 by the LNER and with red lined black livery, during WWII it became simply NE No.1720 and painted plain black. In 1947 it was given a full celebratory makeover of LNER apple green livery as No.8680. By 1949 the engine still retained the green livery but with the addition of the early BR crest. In March 1952 there was a move to full mixed traffic black livery and later in August 1957 the crest was updated. In December 1959 it was updated to plain black, and with poignant significance this engine was withdrawn in October 1961 when wearing its drabbest livery. *H.Forster.*

15

Riddles BR Standard 9F No.92193 of Immingham depot, arrives in platform 8 with a Down parcels train on Saturday 6th June 1959. This engine has been coupled to a BR1F tender and fitted with a double chimney, unusual for an Eastern Region 9F which would normally be fitted with a single chimney. Built at Swindon, the 2-10-0 was put into traffic in May 1958 at Doncaster shed but transferred to Immingham in February 1959 and from where, in June 1965, it was withdrawn somewhat prematurely. At the front of the engine the smokebox hinge straps, dart and number plate border have been smartened up with white paint, a typical Immingham touch which started to have widespread usage throughout BR as the era of the steam locomotive drew to a close. *H.Forster.*

It is the 1st April 1961 and Grantham based Gresley A3 No.60112 ST. SIMON has just arrived on the Down morning parcels train. Fitted with a double chimney in June 1958, this engine was fitted with these small deflectors in November 1959, one of only four of the class to be fitted with them. Rather late in life, in October 1962, the A3 had the German style trough type smoke deflectors fitted during its final General overall at Doncaster. A necessary addition to the class which should have been fitted years before, the deflectors no doubt gave many of the Gresley Pacifics a couple of years extra life. Starting in October 1960, some fifty-five of the A3s got the trough type smoke deflectors fitted over the next couple of years. No.60112 managed to keep active until December 1964 when it was condemned at New England and later sold to a scrap merchant in East Anglia. *H.Forster.*

Looking decidedly filthy in this 17th June 1961 picture, Peppercorn A2 No.60538 VELOCITY of Heaton, is brewing gently with its safety valves just about to lift. This Pacific was one of five of the class fitted with a multi-valve regulator, easily spotted by the unsightly rodding along the boiler. From new No.60538 had been allocated to Gateshead but in May 1960 transferred across the Tyne to Heaton. In October 1961 it moved further north to Tweedmouth where it was condemned a year later. It returned to its birthplace, Doncaster 'Plant' works, for cutting up in May 1963. Note the coupled wheel balance weights on the leading wheel are slightly in advance of the middle and trailing wheels. Who put that electrification warning flash panel alongside the nameplate? Visible to the right of the engine, is a coach end-board propped up in its store. *H.Forster.*

Passing under the magnificent signal gantry at the west end of Newcastle Central station on 18th June 1955, is ex North Eastern Class R, LNER D20, No. 62383. During its last overhaul (Darlington 28th February to 16th April 1955) the engine was coupled with this rebuilt NER tender with flush sides, similar to the LNER Group Standard 3500 gallon tender. The tender was ex No.62380 which had been condemned in late 1954. No.62383 had been allocated to Alnmouth since its transfer from Hull Dairycoates in June 1951 but it had less than two years operation in front of it before it too was condemned and scrapped, aged 50 years. To the rear of the tender, just discernible, is the colour light gantry at the end of the King Edward bridge, a poignant precursor of things to come. *H.Forster.*

Within sight of the western end of the platforms at Central station was the Forth Bank works of Robert Stephenson & Hawthorn, albeit at a lower level to the main line such as in this view. On 6th April 1958 the works had a strange visitor in the shape of former Great Western Railway pannier tank No.3711. The Aberbeeg (86H) based 0-6-0PT, stands in the transfer yard of RS&H awaiting return to the Western Region. Employed to shunt coal wagons on the system north of Newport, Monmouthshire, No.3711 is seen here, with some irony, having just been converted for oil-firing. It had arrived in Newcastle on 5th February and the oil conversion was carried out by an Edinburgh based company. Apparently, according to the contemporary press, the Western Region planned to convert a number of 'Castle' class locomotives to oil firing. After the last oil firing fiasco, in the early days of BR, you would have thought that the BTC had had enough of oil firing. In the event they had and no more was heard of any planned conversions or, as far as this writer is aware, of No.3711 either. Great Western engines, or at least GWR designs, were no strangers to Robert Stephenson & Hawthorns premises because way back in 1951 they built a batch of 94XX class pannier tanks for the Western Region. *H.Forster.*

20

On a cold 21st January 1958, BR Standard class 3MT 2-6-2T No.82027 of Darlington and latterly of Kirkby Stephen, arrives under Newcastle's No.1 signal box with the 2.43 p.m. Saturdays only stopping train from Richmond. It would be useful to see the route of this train from Yorkshire. Turned out from Swindon works in November 1954, No.82027, along with No.82026, went new to Kirkby Stephen. Both moved to Darlington in January 1958 to join Nos.82028 and 82029 which had been at 51A since new in December 1954. All four then spent time at a number of North Eastern Region depots including Scarborough, Malton, York, West Hartlepool, Low Moor and Copley Hill. After considerable periods in store through lack of employment, the four 2-6-2Ts left the NER in September 1963 for Dorset. But, even there the work was becoming thinner on the ground and in September 1964 the gang of four all transferred to Nine Elms for working empty carriage stock to and from Waterloo station until the inevitable end in 1966/67. However, savour this scene with steam, snow and laden skies - you don't see much of that anymore. To the right, leaking steam profusely, is a V2 on a north bound freight. *H.Forster.*

BR Standard 'Clans' were rare in Newcastle even though five of them were allocated just over the hill in Carlisle, at Kingmoor shed. However, in October 1957 four of the class, two from Polmadie Nos.72000, 72002, and two from Kingmoor Nos.72005 and 72006, were transferred to Edinburgh Haymarket shed for appraisal over the ECML and other routes radiating from the Scottish capital. On Saturday 11th January 1958, No.72005 CLAN MACGREGOR has actually arrived from Carlisle and was caught on camera running 'light' past J27 No.65815. Apparently due to an unfavourable response from the Haymarket and Gateshead drivers during the 'trials', all four were returned from whence they came by March 1958. In December 1959 the whole affair was relived when Polmadie sent all five of its 'Clans' 72000-72004 over to Haymarket but they too returned to 66A after four months, the 64B lads having none of it! *H.Forster.*

(opposite) D20 No.62381, makes a spirited start from platform 4 with the 1.20 p.m. Saturdays only to Alnwick, while being photographed by another enthusiast on 26th August 1954. To the right, in platform 2, is a set of LNER-built North Tyneside electric units, which ran from 1936 to 1967. *I.Falcus.*

Rebuilt 'Scot' No.46162 QUEEN'S WESTMINSTER RIFLEMAN, of Saltley depot, arriving at platform 8 on 26th August 1961 with a relief from Birmingham (New Street). This engine was a recent acquisition for Saltley and was one of the better engines in the class. In the background to the right, is a set of 1954-5 built, Newcastle—South Shields, 3rd rail, 2 car electric multiple units, which were to be transferred to the Southern Region in the not too distant future. *I.Falcus.*

(opposite) A magical shot by any standards. An unusually clean Heaton A3, No.60045 LEMBERG, majestically accelerates towards the castle keep in late November 1962. The reason for its reasonable external condition had nothing to do with Heaton shed but more to do with the fact that on Thursday 1st November it had just completed a General overhaul at Doncaster works and, had been repainted in the process. Since January 1937 this Gresley Pacific had been assigned to the North Eastern area and remained so to the end of its life. The second A1 to be rebuilt to A3 standard, LEMBERG completed the process as early as December 1927. *I.Falcus.*

A bunch of indifferent spotters ignore Thompson A2/3 No.60521 WATLING STREET of Heaton, about to depart platform 9 with an Edinburgh—King's Cross relief on Saturday 26th August 1961. At the commencement of the winter timetable in a few weeks hence, the Pacific would move to Tweedmouth where a years employment awaited prior to being withdrawn in November 1962. Stored over the harsh winter months in case of emergency call-up, No.60521 finally took its final journey in May 1963 to Doncaster - just sixteen years old! From this perspective, the straightness of the 'rear' or south wall of Central station is well defined. *I.Falcus.*

A pleasing rear three-quarter view of a Gresley V2. No.60964 THE DURHAM LIGHT INFANTRY of Gateshead shed, arriving at 3.20 p.m. with the Saturdays only parcels train from York on 2nd May 1959. Although diagrammed for a York V2, anything from A4s to B16s could turn up on this working. Together with the 4.30 p.m. stopping passenger service to Berwick, this was the last regular daytime steam turn at Newcastle which lasted until late 1964, and spasmodically into 1965. Note the wrong facing lion on the new BR crest. *I.Falcus.*

The superbly designed W.Worsdell 0-4-4T NER Class O, LNER G5 in the shape of No.67325 of Blaydon shed stands at the head of the 11.50 a.m. service to Hexham on 13th August 1954. The Westinghouse pump is marking time as the engine prepares to depart from platform 12. *I.Falcus*.

Thompson L1 No.67755 of Middlesbrough shed, prepares to take empty coaching stock to Heaton carriage sidings from the rear portion of the Down NORSEMAN on Saturday 30th June 1956. The first coach is part of a triplet restaurant car. In the far distance is J39 No.64703 of Heaton, with the 2.29 p.m. summer Saturdays arrival from Scarborough. *I.Falcus.*

Darlington based and LNER built A5/2 No.69832 arrives at platform 8 with the 2.43 p.m. Saturdays only stopping train from Richmond on 7th September 1957. Shortly after this weekend, the A5 would transfer to Botanic Gardens shed in Hull to begin its last year of operational life. Just above the smokebox is an excellent example of one of the many platform number signs found at Newcastle Central during this period. *I.Falcus.*

A clear rear view of Eastern Region GE Lines 'Britannia' No.70041 SIR JOHN MOORE of Stratford shed, on a summer Saturday King's Cross—Edinburgh service, which the Pacific had hauled from Grantham. This 30th August 1958 visit was the first recorded by a Britannia to Newcastle. *I.Falcus.*

Sunday excursions to Newcastle provided interesting workings in the 1950s. Trains ran every four to six weeks from March to October. For instance, motive power from Hull was usually a Dairycoates B1 or K3, from Leeds it would be a Neville Hill A3, and from both Derby and Manchester, Stanier 'Jubilees', and Class 5s, or BR Standard 5s. The July 1956 photograph shows 'Jubilees' No.45569 TASMANIA from Leeds Holbeck shed, on M880 from Derby, and No.45648 RALEIGH of Kentish Town shed, on W592 from Manchester. Note the 20A shedplate adorning the smokebox door of No.45569 showing that the former LMS depots in the Leeds area were not yet integrated into the North Eastern Region. *I.Falcus.*

Probably a last minute substitution for a failure, Gresley A3 No.60108 GAY CRUSADER of King's Cross shed, is seen arriving on time at platform 8 on Thursday 22nd August 1957 with the Down morning TALISMAN. Diagrammed for a 'Top Shed' A4, the recently ex works A3 was easily up to the job of keeping time with this train. Interestingly another recently ex works A3, No.60035 WINDSOR LAD of Haymarket, took over for the run to Edinburgh. *I.Falcus.*

Peppercorn A1 No.60156 GREAT CENTRAL of King's Cross, seen departing from platform 8 with the inaugural Up service of THE FAIR MAID on Monday 16th September 1957. This train ran from Perth to King's Cross but the title was short lived, as after a year it reverted back to its original name of MORNING TALISMAN, starting once again from Edinburgh rather than Perth. The pre-FAIR MAID morning Edinburgh—King's Cross service, departing Waverley at 7.30 a.m. arrived in London with plenty of time to form the 4.00 p.m. northbound departure Down TALISMAN. The morning London—Edinburgh service likewise got to Waverley in time to form the Up afternoon TALISMAN. Once the name was dropped and THE MORNING TALISMAN revived, the new timings were 7.50 a.m. ex King's Cross and 8.30 a.m. ex Waverley. *I.Falcus.*

Having just been transferred from Tweedmouth to York - note the lack of a shedplate and the coating of grime - Peppercorn A1 No.60147 NORTH EASTERN departs from platform 8 with an express from King's Cross to Edinburgh on Friday 6th September 1963. This engine spent the whole of its short fifteen year life working from depots in the old North Eastern area. *F.Coulton.*

Back to August 1960 now and we see Haymarket A1 No.60160 AULD REEKIE living up to its name just prior to departure with an Edinburgh relief on the Monday 29th. *F.Coulton.*

Having just crossed the Tyne and watched from the British Railways canteen, a Doncaster 9F, No.92201, brings a train of tanks into the environs of Central station on 9th June 1962. On the last leg of its duty, the 2-10-0 was hauling a Gainsborough to Uphall molasses tank train, which was due to change engines at Heaton - a V2 or Pacific would take over for the next leg. The 9F was just three and a half years old on this date and it is incredible that it had just a few months more than that time period before it was scrapped! The building housing the BR Civil Engineers Department (above the Goods Dept.), and adjacent to the west end of Central station, appears from this aspect like the prow of a ship - perhaps the architect had a maritime background. *F.Coulton.*

Doncaster built BR Standard Class 5 No.73161, along with sister engine No.73160, was allocated new to Blaydon shed in February 1957 but within a couple of weeks they had both transferred to Gateshead shed. Initially the pair were sent to Blaydon to work the Newcastle—Carlisle passenger services but their use was curtailed because they did not comfortably fit the turntable at the exNER London Road engine shed in Carlisle. Now, less than fifteen weeks since delivery from Doncaster, No.73161 is standing at platform 8 on 5th June 1957 in a very mucky state - but at least it is steaming well. The train is the 12.07 p.m. service to Colchester, a regular turn for the Gateshead pair, which they took to York via Sunderland. *I.Falcus.*

A west end study on 9th September 1962 with Heaton based A3 No.60088 BOOK LAW arriving with a train from Bristol (Temple Meads), and about to pass one of the Central station pilots supplied by Gateshead, J72 No.68723. The Pacific is by now fitted with the trough type smoke deflectors which, many say, enhanced their appearance. From a drivers point of view they were certainly an improvement. Condemned in October 1963, No.60088 had spent virtually the whole of its thirty-three year existence working from depots situated in the former NER area. On the right can be seen one of the Darlington built Type 2 diesels which, by now, were virtually everywhere in this part of the NE Region. *F.Coulton.*

With freight passing through the goods lines between the arriving and departing passenger trains, Newcastle (Central) station was a very busy place at times. Here at the west end on 14th September 1963, the immaculate North Eastern liveried J72 No.68723 is taking a Gresley kitchen car to platform 15 for loading up with supplies whilst the rear end of a goods trains rumbles by on the right. On the left a 'Peak' Type 4 diesel is sneaking up with a service from Edinburgh. *F.Coulton*.

(opposite) It had just worked in from Edinburgh with a London bound express but Gresley A4 No.60024 KINGFISHER looks as fresh and immaculate as it did when it left Haymarket shed to take up the train at Waverley. The Pacific was photographed making its way to Gateshead depot for servicing on 15th August 1961. Admitted, No.60024 had recently been through Doncaster works for a General overhaul and repaint but that event took place two months before this scene was captured so Haymarket shed was certainly looking after their star performer. In September 1963 Haymarket lost this engine to the former Caledonian shed at Dalry Road shed but within three months St Margarets got hold of it. In March 1965 the A4 transferred to Ferryhill and worked out its final eighteen months of life on the 3-hour Aberdeen—Glasgow expresses - a fitting way to bow out. *F.Coulton*.

The winter of 1962-62 was one of the coldest on record. We all suffered one way or another but British Railways really got hammered. Many of its new diesel locomotives froze up so that stored and even withdrawn steam locomotives had to be resurrected to cover for them. Whatever was the reason behind the unusual appearance of 'Rebuilt Patriot' No.45531 SIR FREDERICK HARRISON of Liverpool's Edge Hill shed on the 3.39 p.m. arrival from Liverpool (Lime Street) on 17th February 1963, it was welcomed by the assembled throng. The wintry conditions didn't deter the young spotters though and for most of them Duffel coats with Wellington boots became the 'dress of the day'! *I.Falcus.*

A warm and sunny Saturday 18th April 1964 at Gateshead Greensfield motive power depot - 52A. The days of the steam locomotive residing here much longer are numbered. Officially 20th March 1965 is the date when the steam allocation was dispersed and effectively banned from the premises but it was to be well into the following October before the last visiting engines used the place for servicing. This fine study of a group outside the Pacific shed includes, front left to right: Thompson B1 No.61322 of Gateshead, Gresley V2 No.60877 of York, Gresley A4 No.60002 SIR MURROUGH WILSON of Gateshead, and WD 2-8-0 No.90506 from Doncaster. Note the length of track discarded to one side, reminiscent of those wartime photographs of depots on mainland Europe after an Allied bombing raid.

15th November 1963 - Gateshead's home based A4 No.60016 SILVER KING, one of the original SILVER JUBILEE quartet, stands on the threshold of the Pacific shed with its mouth agape waiting for attention. Worthy of note is the operating bracket for the handle to open the 'cods' mouth', located just below the valve rod, and in front of the cylinder cover. Details of the AWS gear in front of the bogie can also be seen. Some wag has chalked 'Steam Forever', on both buffer heads. Officially this engine should have transferred to St Margarets shed on Monday 28th October but as can be seen from the shed plate it was still on Gateshead's books or was it? On Sunday 10th November it was to have relocated to Aberdeen Ferryhill, the 64A transfer having been obviously discarded but here we are on Friday 15th with 52A still holding on to it. Strangely, the locomotive is clean, a quite unusual occurrence at Gateshead during this time. Eventually the A4 did move to Scotland and enjoyed more than a year of working the 3-hour Aberdeen—Glasgow expresses before being condemned in March 1965.

That's more like it! Outside the Pacific shed Saturday 9th November 1963 - What a sorry state for a once beautiful locomotive, A4 No.60002 SIR MURROUGH WILSON, at its home depot of Gateshead, with, in similar condition on the adjacent road, B1 No.61238 LESLIE RUNCIMAN from Tyne Dock. This was the typical external presentation of most of Gateshead's engines in the latter days. Just above the B1 can be seen the roof the former depot laundry on Chaytor's Bank. Except for six weeks in 1943, when it was at King's Cross, the A4 had always been at Gateshead engine and managed to keep the same tender throughout its twenty-six year life (T5673) which was one of the non-corridor streamlined types. Within six months its exploits up and down the ECML to London will have been forgotten although this engine was never a regular on the non-stops or post-war streamliners. Sold for scrap in July 1964 it went to a yard at Cargo Fleet.

J72 No.68736, recently transferred from York, and still sporting a 50A shedplate, stands at the back of the ash heaps - the spotters 'covert' entrance to the shed. The date is Saturday 26th October 1963 and behind the engine is the open (roofless) roundhouse with its by now open air turntable. Beyond that is the main depot which had been transformed into a modern diesel depot, albeit utilising the walls of the former roundhouses along with numerous pre-cast concrete beams. Originally there was four roundhouses here, all in a line running south-west to north-east, the now open air shed being No.4 with a 60ft turntable. Nos.3 and 2 sheds were converted for the diesels whilst No.1 shed was removed to create a yard outside. Visible to the right, is the north wall of the Pacific shed.

About to reverse out of the depot to take a train south on 7th December 1963, is Peppercorn A1 No.60141 ABBOTSFORD of York. This engine, when allocated to Leeds Copley Hill shed, was an extremely rare visitor in the north-east. The wall behind the Pacific was the reconstructed No.2 roundhouse which now housed the Gateshead diesel fleet. To the right can be seen, at the front of that new depot, a BR Brush-Sulzer Type 4 diesel-electric D1527 which was allocated to Finsbury Park. The Co-Co diesel was handed over to British Railways in June 1963, one of thirty-three delivered 34G. Gateshead had to wait until April 1964 before its first allocation of the type (D1574 to D1582) arrived from Crewe works. It was to be another eighteen months before the next and final batch of new Brush Type 4s were allocated (D1977 to D1989), again these were Crewe built. Back to our subject locomotive, from here the A1 could gain direct access to Newcastle (Central) by either reversing on the same course out over the King Edward bridge and backing straight onto its southbound train, or by proceed forward over the High Level bridge passing through the station and then backing onto its train. Any turning was done at either of the available triangles on this bank of the river.

The remnants of Gateshead's demolished No.4 roundhouse, is home to a trio of British Railways built J72s Nos.69023, 69025 and 69028 on 7th December 1963. Worthy of note is the new brick built gable end, an addition to the existing stone work of what is the new diesel depot. The stone walls are remnants of the 1867 built No.3 roundhouse with the arched connections into this later, circa 1877, built roundhouse. What remained of the lives of these three 0-6-0Ts was quite different for each engine. No.69023 became Departmental No.59 on 26th October 1964 when it moved on to North Blyth. No.69025 was condemned three weeks after this scene was recorded. It was later sold for scrap after languishing derelict for a year. No.69028 hung on at Gateshead for another ten months work, mainly at Central station but doing other jobs too. It was purchased by the same scrap merchant as No.69025, T.J.Thompson of Stockton and the condemned pair travelled to Teesside coupled together. No.59 lasted until September 1966 when it was purchased for preservation.

A yard shot from 9th November 1963 showing recently arrived A4 No.60002 SIR MURROUGH WILSON. Stabled adjacent to the water tower is one of the large BR Type 4 diesels which eventually became Class 46 under the TOPS scheme. Gateshead had a large number of these 1-Co Co-1 diesel locomotives long before steam was banished from the premises. Between May 1962 and January 1963, Derby built Nos.D166 to D193 arrived and took over the Newcastle—Liverpool (Lime St.) and Newcastle—West of England express passenger trains. Besides those workings they also did their share on the ECML to Edinburgh (Waverley) and London (King's Cross) although the latter place did not see too much of them in comparison. When the Class 46 diesels began to be withdrawn during the early 1980s, nearly all of the class had migrated to Gateshead depot - by then a sort of spiritual home. The water tower formed the eastern end of the manual coaling stage and the line of the roof can be made out with the aid of the whitewashed brickwork. The buildings in the background are part of the former locomotive works.

The sleek lines of Gresley V2 No.60962, one of Gateshead's own, can be seen as it awaits its next turn of duty at the front of the Pacific shed on 11th January 1964. To the right, V3 tanks congregate around the turntable roads of the erstwhile No.4 roundhouse. The-three road Pacific shed was at one time at part of the Gateshead locomotive works, in use as a tender shop. The Running Department took over shortly after Grouping when it was also extended at this, its eastern end. The use of this straight shed for the LNER's Pacific locomotives stems from the fact that none of the roundhouse then in use at Gateshead had 70ft turntables, the minimum requirement for the Gresley and Raven engines. The largest turntables available inside were only 60ft. in diameter. So, the LNER deemed it cheaper, and more practical, to convert this building for locomotive use. And so it remained until steam was banished from the depot in October 1965 which was about the time when the V2 was condemned. The Pacific shed was demolished in 1969 and so ended another chapter in the history of steam traction.

On a very cold Saturday 18th January 1964, the frost covered hulk of 'Britannia' Pacific No.70013 OLIVER CROMWELL, complete with nameplates, is flanked by a locally based 'Peak' and Deltic D9005 THE PRINCE OF WALE'S OWN REGIMENT OF YORKSHIRE. The 'Brit' is recently out of store at March shed and, minus connecting rods, is in transit to Kingmoor shed having been transferred from the Eastern Region. It will reside at Gateshead depot until Monday morning, and then be towed dead to Carlisle to begin a short but glorious four-year career. The 'Britannias' were never regular visitors to Tyneside but many of the former ER examples found their way to Kingmoor via the ECML and Gateshead. Note the state of the trackwork which no doubt required some very slow running through the yard to prevent derailments. The line on which the 'Peak' stands appears to have some kind of temporary obstruction lay across the rails.

Being checked out by a fitter on Saturday 26th October 1963, is locally based Gresley 2-6-2T V3 No.67640, stabled on one of the open turntable roads of No.4 shed. This is a good detailed shot showing the plated coal rail bunker, the North British destination board brackets, footsteps on the bunker side and the sight screens on the side of the cab. In the background one of Gateshead's diesel mechanical 0-6-0 shunters occupies the 60ft turntable.

A smoky picture of two east coast giants - Peppercorn A1 No.60129 GUY MANNERING of Tweedmouth shed, and Deltic D9015 TULYAR from Finsbury Park. The date is 24th January 1964 and although its lamps have yet to be set, the Pacific is about to make its way to Newcastle (Central) to take up an early afternoon northbound working. The yard lighting is still somewhat rudimentary with single bulb illumination atop wooden telegraph poles. Illumination was something BR never addressed during steam days except at the larger marshalling yards. Engine sheds therefore were fairly dangerous places without traffic movement and night visits to sheds had to be undertaken with extreme care if the ashpits and inspection pits were to be avoided. A V2 and an English Electric Type 4 complete the picture.

Until 1965 this engine was always number one in the Eastern Region Ian Allan ABC. Gresley A4 No.60001 SIR RONALD MATTHEWS is at its home depot - 52A Gateshead on 7th February 1964. This is a fine study of a streamlined non-corridor tender (No.T5674) which had been coupled to this engine throughout its life. Only this tender and that behind No.60002 (No.T5673), had the thick plated strip along the bottom edge. The A4 is now in its last year of life and by October it will have been laid up and put in store. On the twelfth day of that month it was condemned and awaited a buyer for its hundred plus tons of joined-up metal.

The sad sight of A4 No.60020 GUILLEMOT, being towed away on the 11th April 1964 by an unidentified but unmistakably filthy WD 2-8-0 to Darlington works, after having been withdrawn the previous month. The A4 had been cleaned but not its life-long tender (No.T5669), which still contained a reasonable supply of coal, suggesting that the locomotives demise had been all rather sudden. On arrival at Darlington shed, prior to works acceptance, the Pacific was kept waiting for a couple of weeks before the order arrived to dismantle the once proud 'Streak'. As LNER No.4465, GUILLEMOT was a regular performer on the pre-war SILVER JUBILEE streamliner. Contractors are working in the yard of the diesel depot but what was being erected at this time is unknown. Note the state of the trackwork around this area - subsidence, the different levels and gradients in all directions.

Heading for Stella South power station, a heavily laden coal train passes Gateshead shed on 14th March 1964, with Raven Q6 No.63431 of Tyne Dock shed in charge. In the background English Electric Type 4s and the Derby built Brush-Sulzer Type 4s stable in the drizzle at the east end of the depot. This photograph was taken from Chaytors Bank where locomotives were often stored during British Railways days; before Nationalisation the five stabling roads would sometimes be used as an overflow for Greensfield engine shed. In the mid distance can be seen the roof of a now abandoned roundhouse which was once used by the locomotive works as a paint shop. However, the building was opened at some time during the 1860s by the North Eastern as an engine shed, predating the last two roundhouses at Greensfield. Before Grouping the wonderfully shaped building had been converted from its intended role into a paint shop for the works but even that activity had long ceased by 1964. Demolition took place not long after this Saturday morning event took place. I suppose that today the roundhouse would have become a listed building but in the Gateshead of the 1960s it was all about renewal of the urban landscape.

Arriving light engine onto the depot on 11th April 1964, and followed by an English Electric Type 4 diesel, York based Gresley V2 No.60847, without nameplates, was formerly named ST. PETER'S SCHOOL, YORK, A.D.627. The engine is framed by one of the 'gallowed' signal gantries which were so profuse around this area and of which three are visible in this picture. From new in March 1939, the V2 had spent most of its life working from York shed although for the summer timetable of 1946 it was allocated to Neville Hill. At its last General overhaul in late 1961, No.60847 received the separate cylinder layout which many of the class were then being fitted, albeit some might say, a bit late in the day. At the same repair a speedometer was also fitted and that can be made out projecting from the rear coupled wheel. Having started life at York the 2-6-2 finished it there and was withdrawn on Tuesday 29th June 1965. It was sold for scrap during August to a Midlands based company.

On Saturday 18th April 1964, between duties, Blaydon based Thompson B1 No.61322 was standing outside the Pacific shed at Gateshead depot. The proximity of the running lines to the King Edward Bridge can be seen veering off to the right behind the shed whilst behind the B1 was the lean-to wooden building which housed the Gateshead breakdown crane. Evidence that an earlier building was attached to the Pacific shed can be seen by the markings running parallel with the roof line. The girder - rolled steel joist - was put in when the shed was initially converted from a tender shop and replaced the original three brick arches. Before the King Edward bridge connection was put in, the area to the left of the shed contained four sidings of which only this one remained, although the NER Locomotive Running Dept. would not have been using the sidings in the pre-Grouping period. On the other side of the Pacific shed was the erstwhile Redheugh branch which ran the full length of the shed yard between the roundhouses to the north and this straight shed on the south side. But, the branch was long closed by the time the engine sheds were being expanded and the original alignment was incorporated into the yard.

At home on 18th April 1964 and standing in front of the Pacific shed, with the revamped main shed building in the background, is a beautiful but rather grubby Gresley A4 No.60002 SIR MURROUGH WILSON. Mention earlier of the thick bottom plate on the tender draws your eyes to that area which appears to have suffered some recent collision damage. Within a few weeks of this quiet event being 'snapped' for posterity, the big engine was condemned. It was long overdue a major overhaul and that wasn't going to happen so it was consigned to scrap at a private yard in Cargo Fleet.

A rather pleasing shot of Gresley A3 No.60051 BLINK BONNY of Darlington, standing outside the Pacific shed on Saturday 25th April 1964. The view shows, in detail, the rear of the new type tender, including the protection plate behind the coupling to prevent the vacuum cylinder from being damaged. Inside the Pacific shed whitewashed walls aided the austere and meagre lighting hanging from the rafters of the high roof. In the absence of a suitable turntable of the correct diameter, the triangles at Gateshead East and West junctions were used for turning Pacific locomotives. On the V2 to the right of the picture, can be seen the speedometer drive cable.

Inside the Pacific shed on 2nd May 1964 with A4 No.60001 prominent. With no proper ventilation installed in what was essentially a running shed, rather than repair shop, it is wonder that the LNER and later BR got away with using this place as they did. Obviously the high roof helped but nevertheless any excess smoking would have quickly made this building a very unhealthy place to be. A certain amount of repair went on in the shed and the wheel drop was used judging by the number of leaf springs on the floor and against the south wall. Note that the A4 is rather clean - at least for a 52A engine.

On the other side of the Pacific shed that day, with its bogie over the wheel drop, filthy Gresley A3 No.60071 TRANQUIL, is awaiting an examination. This Pacific had been a Gateshead engine since June 1963, almost a year, but it still has not had a shed plate fitted. No. doubt the rapidly increasing 52A diesel fleet were having theirs fitted and the shortage, if there was one, stemmed from the fact that each diesel required two shed plates! No.60071 had spent much of its life allocated to Gateshead shed both as an A1 and A3. Certainly it had spent the whole of its life at North Eastern Area depots. However, nothing lasts for ever and on 12th October 1964 this engine was condemned and by Christmas it was in a very (in)famous scrapyard in Hull. The acetylene gear in the foreground was probably used to remove stubborn nuts.

Saturday 30th May 1964. Working hard on a civil engineers train while passing Hoggetts crisp factory, just to the west of Gateshead shed, is Peppercorn K1 No.62024. As an added aside Hoggetts crisps were the finest I've ever tasted.

POTATO CRISPS

62024

A neat rear end shot of Peppercorn A1 No.60155 BORDERER, backing off the depot and passing the Pacific shed, while heading for Newcastle (Central). This was one of the five A1s fitted with roller bearings and was reputed to be one of the finest "blue 'ns", according to Gateshead driver Andy Robson, a reference to the high esteem in which the A1s were held from when they were first allocated in blue livery to Gateshead. Clearly can be seen the position of the electric lighting conduit on the back of the tender, which varied from engine to engine. Steam is escaping from the train heating hose and shows up well in this 19th December 1964 illustration.

A well lit shot of the otherwise gloomy interior of the Pacific shed on 7th February 1964 looking towards the wheel drops. Centre stage is Gresley A3 and local boy No.60091 CAPTAIN CUTTLE. Just getting into frame from the left is Peppercorn A1 No.60124 KENILWORTH from York, which appears to have had a bump, as the buffer and front bufferbeam are bent out at a 45 degree angle. Normally during this period in the lead up to the end of steam a locomotive sustaining such damage would have been condemned but the A1 was due a visit to Darlington works anyway so six days after this scene was recorded No.60124 entered the shops at Darlington and was given a General overhaul. The repair actually took three months to complete but nevertheless it was done and the Pacific came back into traffic in mid May. In December 1965 and by now allocated to Darlington shed, the A1 was involved in yet another minor bump requiring a visit to works. Once again it escaped with a Casual Light repair and returned to traffic in January 1966. Eventually its luck ran out and on Sunday 27th March 1966 it was condemned and later sold for scrap. Towards the back of this image are a tenderless V2 over the wheel drop, and a Thompson B1.

A pleasing shot of Gresley V3 67620 being turned on 30th May 1964 by the 60ft electric table of the erstwhile No.4 shed. A sorry looking Drewry shunter D2249 lies to the left and J72 No.69005 is behind.

(opposite) On the same May day in 1964 the last BR built J72, No.69028, sun bathes in the corner of the roofless roundhouse waiting for its next job. The turntables inside the North Eastern Railway roundhouses were once all boarded over for safety reasons (If there had been a H&SE in those days the NER would have got a pat on the back for that one) and the remnants of the steel joists on which the boards sat are still in situ on this table, the boards however have long gone. But steel railings now feature to stop anyone falling into the pit. The stone walls are quite substantial and at a quick glance could virtually pass for casements in a fort of the Napoleonic period, the grills in the window however, have more of a Victorian period prison look about them.

It is 20th June 1964 and Darlington based K1 No.62043, on a mixed freight train heading east, is passing the old roundhouse at Chaytors Bank and at the same time is framed beautifully by the interesting details of the footbridge at the east end of the depot. The crossing in the foreground leads to Gateshead West station and the lines to the right lead into the depot via the coaling stage, those tracks are a remnant of the long gone Redheugh branch and were latterly used by engines which required turning on the east triangle before they came on shed.

A busy image of the line between Greensfield, Gateshead engine shed and Chaytors Bank on 20th June 1964. J27 No.65791 of Blyth is passing along the Up main line whilst Peppercorn K1 No.62026 from Gateshead is working along the Down branch towards Felling. Note the skeletal and glassless conical roof atop the 1862-built Chaytors Bank roundhouse. During route widening in the early period of the 20th Century, a small section of the roundhouse, affecting three of the twenty pitched roof bays, was cut back and the resulting repair to the wall created a flat face which, in plan form would have appeared like a flat tyre on an otherwise perfect circular building. The view of the roundhouse on the opposite page reveals the reworked area above the tender of the K1 and the first van of its train. To the far left of this frame we can just see a tiger-striped 350hp 0-6-0 diesel shunter negotiating the Down main. Surprisingly Gateshead never got any of these locomotives newly delivered and those which subsequently reached the allocation (seven by June 1964) were second-hand from other depots. Of the smaller 200 h.p. 0-6-0 BR and Drewry diesel mechanical shunters however, 52A could boast to having twenty on the strength at this time in 1964 and most of those had come to Gateshead new from the makers at either Robert, Stephenson & Hawthorn, or BR Doncaster.

Resting on 'the ash heaps' at the extreme western end of the depot on 20th June 1964, and accompanied by a pair of independent snow ploughs, is Gresley V3 No.67690. By now the V3s at Gateshead were not exactly over employed and No.67690, along with Nos.67620, 67628, 67646, and 67691, which had all arrived at the depot in the previous eighteen months, were destined for withdrawal before the end of the year. No.67690 escaped to Darlington shed in mid October whilst the others remained at 52A but 'the writing was on the wall' for these last remnants of the V3 class. On Monday 23rd November they were all condemned and later sold for scrap to a yard in Stockton - the V3 class was extinct nearly two years after their cousins in Class V1 had also become extinct. The birds flying out of shot to the left, are some of Gateshead's more unusual 'residents'. Those pigeons lived in pigeon crees (or duckets) built between the two lines leading to the King Edward Bridge (known as the west triangle), and were regularly seen swirling and swooping to and fro in perfect unison.

With the fireman ready to dismount to change the points, the strong and powerful lines of BR Standard 9F No.92201 of Doncaster, fitted with a type 1F tender, can be seen in this 15th August 1964 view in the shed yard. For modellers purposes this is a useful picture, as it clearly displays the details on the rear of the tender.

Stabled at the east end of the depot on Saturday 30th May 1964 is a Gateshead based Brush Type 4 D1582 with an unidentified BR Sulzer Type 4 alongside. Looking rather smart in its two-tone green livery, D1582 had arrived new from Crewe works just a few days previously, the last of a batch of nine (Nos. D1574 to D1582) to be allocated to 52A during April and May 1964. No more examples of this class, which became 47 under the TOPS scheme, came new until another Crewe built batch arrived during the period from December 1965 to February 1966 (Nos. D1977 to D1989). By then of course steam was long gone from the depot and the age of the diesels had really started at Gateshead Traction Maintenance Depot. The building to the extreme right of the picture was the oldest railway hotel in the world, which although Grade II listed, was sadly and possibly wrongly demolished when the Ochre Yards housing complex was built on the site of the former depot in 2006 - the ghost of TDS still haunts Tyneside.